CHILDREN AS ARROWS

DUANE SHERIFF

CHILDREN AS ARROWS

Navigating Parenthood with Scriptural Wisdom

Duane Sheriff

COPYRIGHT

All rights reserved. No portion of this book may be reproduced, stored in a retrieval system, or transmitted in any form or by any means (electronic, mechanical, photocopy, recording, scanning, etc.) without prior written consent of the publisher.

Scriptures quoted in this book are used by permission and referenced within using the following abbreviations:

Unless noted otherwise, all Scripture quotations are from *The New King James Version.* Copyright 1982 by Thomas Nelson. Used by permission. All rights reserved.

The *King James Edition* of the Bible (KJV). 1987 Public Domain in the United States of America.

The *New Living Translation* (NLT) The Holy Bible, New Living Translation, copyright 1996, 2004, 2007 by Tyndale House Foundation. Used by permission of Tyndale House Publishers, Inc., Carol Stream, Illinois 60188. All rights reserved.

The *Amplified Bible, Classic Edition* (AMPC) Copyright 1954, 1958, 1962, 1964, 1965, 1987 by The Lockman Foundation Used by permission. www.Lockman.org

Scripture quotations marked TPT are from *The Passion Translation*®. Copyright © 2017, 2018, 2020 by Passion & Fire Ministries, Inc. Used by permission. All rights reserved. ThePassionTranslation.com.

Scripture quotations marked BSB are taken from the Berean Standard Bible © 2016 by Bible Hub and Berean.Bible. Used by permission. All rights reserved.

All emphasis within Scripture quotations is the author's own.

Printed in the United States of America.
© 2024 by Victory Life Church
PO Box 427
Durant, OK 74702
dsm@pastorduane.com
580.634.5665

CONTENTS

INTRODUCTION		1
Chapter 1	PARENTS AS WATCHMEN	3
Chapter 2	ARROWS	10
Chapter 3	GODLY SEED	23
Chapter 4	TRAINING WITH THE ROD	30
Chapter 5	PROVOKE NOT TO WRATH	46
Chapter 6	TEACHING	55
Chapter 7	FOUNDATIONS BY ADULTHOOD	67
Chapter 8	DIFFERENT KINDS OF LOVE	80
Chapter 9	GOD'S KIND OF LOVE	87
Chapter 10	BLESSING OUR CHILDREN	100

INTRODUCTION

Like arrows in the hand of a warrior, so are the children of one's youth.

Psalm 127:4

The biblical illustration of children as arrows is a beautiful and apt description of healthy parent-child relationships. Like a master craftsman builds and shapes an arrow for battle, so God gives children into our care to prepare them for their future. But notice they are *"arrows in the hand of a warrior"* (Psalm 127:4). Whether or not you recall the application you completed before becoming a mom or dad, parenting is not for the faint of heart. It is a battle. And wimps need not apply!

Everything in our culture wars against the family; it wars against parents. But as an arrow is designed to accurately hit a specific target, so parents are assigned to protect, prepare, and propel children into their futures despite the fallen world in which we live. Our children are made to prosper, and we, as parents, are designed to succeed in our calling.

But that success doesn't happen by accident. It requires partnership with the One who gave them.

Psalm 127:3 says, *"Children are a heritage **from** the Lord, the fruit of the womb is a reward."* Heritage here simply means gift. Our children are gifts from God. They did not come from us; they came through us. God entrusts our children to us and partners with us as we raise them in the nurture of the Lord (Ephesians 6:4). Psalm 127:5 says, *"Happy is the man who has his quiver full of them."* Yet many people quiver with just one! They wonder what sin they committed in a previous life to be punished with such strong-willed, misbehaving children, and they don't even believe in reincarnation! Dear ones, that is not what parenting is supposed to feel like. God wants our family life to be a mutual blessing for us and our children. And He has a plan to accomplish it. In this book, we'll cover simple, foundational truths from God's word that will equip us for the journey (and sometimes fight) of parenting. But this fight is a good fight—one where God is truly on our side. Let's enjoy the ride!

Chapter 1 | PARENTS AS WATCHMEN

Unless the Lord builds the house, they labor in vain who build it. Unless the Lord guards the city, the watchman stays awake in vain. It is vain for you to rise up early, to sit up late, to eat the bread of sorrows; for so he gives His beloved sleep.

Psalm 127:1-2

It is vain to try and raise our children independent of partnership with God. We can't do it. We lose sleep and eat the bread of sorrows. Parenting independent of God is a self-destructive mission.

Building a family, like building a house, requires certain skills. It requires foundational truths that only God can provide. We are watchmen over our children. God won't raise them independent of us, and it is extremely unwise for us to try and raise them independent of Him. But with God's engagement—His help and instruction—we can fulfil our appointment as parents. We don't need to worry about our children. We don't need to be filled with anxiety over them. We can cast our care on the Lord, for He genuinely cares for us (I Peter 5:7). God wants us to experience peace as we serve as watchman over our children's lives.

The key is balance. Proverbs 11:1 (KJV) says, *"A false balance is an admonition to the Lord: But a just weight is his delight."* We can get in a ditch on either side of the road regarding our ministry as parents and the best method for effective parenting. Some parents are disengaged. They do not understand the importance of being a watchman for their kids. They allow digital media to raise them, and the wolves and lions of this world devour their children. Others are "helicopter parents." They smother their children, even into adulthood. They try to control them through manipulation and worry. We need to stay out of both those ditches. Remember, for every mile of road traveled, there is a mile of ditch on both sides. That makes two miles of ditches for every mile of wisdom and understanding. Only through partnership with God and His Word can we stay balanced.

The first thing we need to know to maintain this balance as watchmen over our families, is that God loves our kids. His heart is for us. It is for our families. Children are near and dear to God's heart. Do you realize, the only thing God did not create independent of man is children. Think about that! Everything God created He created in maturity. There was no baby Adam or Eve. They were created full grown, mature adults who could be "fruitful and multiply" (Genesis 1:26-28). It's as if God didn't want to raise teenagers. (I can see the wisdom in that!) Even the promised Messiah came through partnership with man. Mary had to believe before she could receive the promised seed and bring forth the Holy Child, Jesus (Luke 1:26-38).

We see God's love for children throughout Scripture. In Matthew 18 the disciples asked Jesus a question: *"At the same time came the disciples unto Jesus, saying, who is the greatest in the kingdom of Heaven? And Jesus called a **little child** unto him, and set him in the midst of them, and said, Verily I say unto you, except ye be converted, and become as **little children**, ye shall not enter into the kingdom of heaven. Whosoever therefore shall humble* *himself as this* **little child**, *the same is greatest in the kingdom of heaven"* (Matthew 18:1-4, KJV). Think about their question: Who is the greatest in God's kingdom? What would we say? A preacher or TV evangelist with a large following? Maybe a missionary who gave their life on a foreign field? Perhaps they thought Jesus would single out one of them. But look at the answer Jesus gave—A child.

Children are full of faith and humility. They are eager to learn, eager to believe. Their imagination is unparalleled. Children believe animals talk, rabbits lay eggs, and reindeer fly. They believe in Santa Claus, the Tooth Fairy, and Leprechauns. Children have to be taught to disbelieve. Part of our job as watchmen is to protect a child's natural ability to believe. Childlike faith reminds us that *"all things are possible to him who believes"* (Matthew 17:20 & 19:26, Mark 9:23). Children encourage us to set aside doubt, to forget about probability or natural law and "believe only" (Mark 5:36, Luke 8:50). They inspire us to believe that miracles still happen and that God is a good Father who delights in meeting His children's needs (Romans 8:32).

We are also called to protect children's moral innocence. Luke 17 says, *"There will always be temptations to sin, but what sorrow awaits the person who does the tempting. It would be better to be thrown into the sea with a millstone hung around your neck then to cause one of these little ones to fall into sin."* (Luke 17:2, NLT).

Our culture sets stumbling blocks before children every day. Yet, I am appalled at the number of people who are not just inviting children to sin but are taking pleasure in pulling them into sin. I grieve over what they are doing. Recently, while in Israel, I saw an ancient millstone. It was huge! Its diameter was nearly as tall as I am. Can you imagine something that size pulling you into the depths of the sea? I cannot think of a more horrific death, or a more fitting judgment for harming a child. As watchmen, we must protect our children from the death and darkness of the world. We must honor God's love for children, for they are special.

INTRODUCING JESUS

One of the ways we do this is by introducing our children to Jesus while they are still young. As parents, we are called to train and teach our children in "the way" of righteousness (Ephesians 6:4, Deuteronomy 32:46-47). We are not teaching them "a way," nor the world's way. We are instructing them in God's way. We are teaching them righteousness and justice from God's perspective. Consider why God chose Abraham to be the father of our faith (Genesis 12:1-3). God could have chosen anyone—Abel, Enoch, Noah, or others. But there was something different about Abraham. Something that drew God's eye:

> *"And the Lord said, 'Shall I hide from Abraham what I am doing, since Abraham shall surely become a great and mighty nation and all the nations of the earth shall be blessed in him? For I have known him, in order **that he may command his children and his household after him**, that they **keep the way of the Lord, to do righteousness and justice**, that the Lord may bring to Abraham what He has spoken to him."*
>
> Genesis 18:17-19

God saw Abraham's faith. He knew him. He knew Abraham would not just maintain his own faith, he would command his children and household to keep the way of the Lord. Abraham would protect his children from darkness and introduce them to the Light. He would think generationally. He would be a righteous watchman over his home.

Our God is a generational God. He is the God of Abraham, Isaac, and Jacob. And He works generationally. If we are of the faith of Abraham, we too must think generationally. We must watch over our household (our children and grandchildren) to teach them the way of the Lord. God has entrusted us with our children. May we be found trustworthy to pass on the faith, to teach them "the way, truth, and life," while they are young and humble of heart, while it is easy to believe (John 14:6). For our children came from God, and they will return to Him through Jesus Christ.

Chapter 2 | ARROWS

Children are a heritage from the Lord; the fruit of the womb is a reward.

Psalm 127:3

Before we break down the illustration of children as arrows, I want to remind us all: There are no perfect parents. Neither are there perfect children. We live in a fallen world. But that is exactly why we need God. Without Him, parenthood is a heavy weight not a reward. Sue and I were not perfect parents, nor did God give us perfect kids. Yet He was faithful to us in the raising of them. And we took comfort in the thought that even God—the perfect parent—who created two perfect adults, and placed them into a perfect world, did not see perfect results.

Adam and Eve chose to disobey God's Word and plunged the universe into darkness, sin, and death (Genesis 3:1-6, Romans 5:12). Though He was the only innocent party in their sin, God did not forsake them. He loved them. While there were still consequences to Adam's sin, God remained faithful. He promised to send a Deliverer to rescue mankind and bruise Satan's head. God wasn't condemned over His children's actions. And neither should we be condemned if our adult children choose to disobey. God will remain faithful—both to us, as imperfect parents, and to our children. He will not neglect His Word.

People often ask if I have any regrets over parenthood. Would I have done things differently had I known then what I know now? But that's the thing. I didn't know then what I know now. No one does! Sue and I acted in faith then, as we are acting in faith now. And God is blessing us now, as He did then. So, no. We have no regrets. Did we make mistakes? Absolutely! But because we loved God and our children, and were faithful to our purpose as parents, God worked all things together for our family's good (Romans 8:28).

Raising children is messy business. But God's grace is sufficient in our human weakness, and He delights in bringing beauty out of ashes (2 Corinthians 12:9, Isaiah 61:3). Trust God to encourage you as you encourage your children in the ways of the Lord. We also hope you'll allow Sue and I to encourage you with this image of children as arrows.

In the construction of an arrow, there are three obvious sections—the tip, the shaft, and the feathers. Each section serves a specific purpose, but all must work together for the arrow to experience success. The same is true of our children. There are three stages in child development (and thus child rearing) that must work together to successfully launch them into the world—training, teaching, and transition. Our job as parents is to recognize the unique stage our children are in and make the most of every opportunity while they are still in our care (Ephesians 5:15-17). Later chapters of this book will unpack the stages of child rearing in more detail.

FEATHERS   SHAFT   TIP

The three parts of the arrow also provide a useful picture to keep our parenting grounded in God's purposes. As parents, we must remember that our kids are uniquely designed for God-given purposes, given to us for a limited season of childrearing, and should be established in the ways of the Lord.

The tip of an arrow is designed to hit a specific target. This speaks to the individual destiny of each of our children. Our children were created for a purpose (Jeremiah 29:11). Each of them has a divine design, with gifts and personalities, that match God's plan and purpose for their lives. Part of our job as parents is to help them discover those gifts and learn to submit to the leading of the Holy Spirit, so they can take aim at their God-given purpose.

The shaft of an arrow determines its length. This correlates to the length of time God gives children into our care—20 years. In that time, we need to train them to submit to God (through obedience to us), teach them the way of the Lord and prepare them for life outside our home, and then transition them into adulthood fully equipped to follow God and succeed in life. After 20 years, they are adults and responsible (and accountable to God) for their own decisions and choices.

An arrow's feathers are for accuracy. Feathers guide an arrow through turbulent winds ensuring that arrow hits its target. Without feathers an arrow's trajectory is unpredictable. It could harm others or even put itself at risk. This speaks to the spiritual principles we teach our children that guide them through difficult circumstances and keep them rooted in God's love. Without these governing truths, our children will miss God's purpose for their lives. They could also end up harming themselves or others. Let's look at each of these correlating stages more closely.

STAGES AND AGES

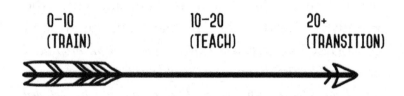

0-10 (TRAIN)   10-20 (TEACH)   20+ (TRANSITION)

There are three stages of development in every child's life: childhood, adolescence, and adulthood. As parents, our role evolves through these stages. In childhood, we are focused on training and protection. In adolescence, our role shifts to teaching, and as our children approach adulthood, we transition them out of our care. We become friends and fulltime cheerleaders. Before adulthood, we are not our child's friend. We are guardians and watchmen.

Scripturally speaking, children are considered adults at 20 years of age. Twenty-year-olds in the Bible were required to pay the temple tax and go to war with the other adults (Exodus 30:14, Numbers 1:18-42). They were also held accountable for their sin. In Numbers 14, God told the Israelites that those 20 and older would die in the wilderness because they refused to trust Him and enter the Promised Land. The people murmured and complained against the Lord: *"You will all drop dead in this wilderness! Because you complained against me, every one of you who is twenty years old or older and was included in the registration will die […] The only exceptions will be Caleb son of Jephunneh and Joshua son of Nun"* (vs. 29-30, NLT). Those under 20 were considered "children" and not held accountable to God for their sin.

TRAINING

Training is the stage of childhood from zero to approximately ten years of age. This is the protective stage of parenthood. In it, we train our children to obey according to Ephesians 6: *"Children, obey your parents in the Lord, for this is right. Honor your father and mother, which is the first commandment with promise: that it may be well with you, and you may live long on the earth"* (vs. 1-3). Though there is some teaching that happens in these years, the focus is training. Proverbs 22:6 tells us to *"Train up a child in the way he should go and when he is old, he will not depart from it."* The word child is significant in this passage. According to Strongs Concordance, it is the "age of infancy to adolescence" (Strongs H5288). But notice, we are to train children. There is a difference between training and teaching. Training involves repetition and consistency. It uses discipline, affirmation, and reward to instill good habits and life skills.

We don't teach lions to jump through hoops or killer whales to perform on demand. We train them. The same is true for children. We don't "teach" life skills once. We train them. (That's why it's called "potty training" not "potty teaching.") From birth to at least eight, we hover over every action and decision children make. We are helicopter parents. "Don't eat that!" "Don't touch that!" "Don't scratch that!" "Don't pick that!" "Be careful." "Look both ways." "Hold my hand; stay close." We set boundaries for their safety and healthy growth, and when they function within those boundaries, we affirm their choices. "Good job!" "I'm proud of you!" "You are precious." "That was awesome." We may even offer rewards for their obedience and accomplishments. The key to training is consistency and discipline. What we ask of our children can't be wrong today but okay tomorrow. The consequences of their actions need to be consistent, which means we, as parents, must be diligent. Training children in these early years is a never-ending job.

TEACHING

Teaching takes place during adolescence, between the ages of eight and ten to twenty. This stage of childhood covers the honor part of Ephesians 6: *"Honor your father and mother, which is the first commandment with promise"* (vs. 2). It is the preparation stage. Proverbs says, *"My son, hear the instruction of your father, and do not forsake the law of your mother. For they will be a graceful ornament on your head and chains about your neck"* (vs. 1:8-9). The word son is significant in this passage. It is a different Hebrew word than what we saw in Proverbs 22:6. This word means "youth" (Strongs, H1121). This is the adolescent stage of childhood. A time is coming when our children will no longer be under our direct authority and will be responsible for their own decisions, but it is not yet.

The adolescent stage is an important time of teaching and preparation for life. During this time, we prepare our children for marriage, for their future career (not necessarily specific skills, but helping them develop a good work ethic, teaching them to process persecution properly, to get along with unbelievers, etc.), and life in general. We teach them the principles and ways of the Lord: how to be responsible for their actions, and accountable before God by focusing on character development, integrity building, and healthy habits so they can be productive adults. During this time, we explain the *why* of obedience. We teach them how to trust God and submit to His Word in all things because we will not always be there. But what we teach them during childhood will follow them all the days of their lives (Proverbs 4:13).

TRANSITION

As our children approach 20, we enter the stage of transition. We have protected them through childhood and prepared them for life during adolescence; now, we are to propel them into their future, equipped to succeed. By the time our children are 20, we should have resigned from "helicopter parenting" and laid down our role as "teacher." Now we fill the role of friend and counselor (when asked).

By this time, our children should be prepared for adulthood. They should know how to take responsibility for their actions, serve God and their families, and have a good work ethic. They should know they were created on purpose and with a purpose. They should be a giver, not a taker, serving others rather than being a drag on society. They need to know the basics of love—the intentional, Godkind of love that chooses to give freely of itself rather than be served through temporal feelings. This knowledge prepares them to have happy, healthy marriages, and to be good parents for the next generation. Titus 2:4 tells us that this kind of love is taught, not caught: *"These older women must train the younger women to love their husbands and their children"* (NLT).

Our children also need to know how to find and fulfill God's will for their life. By 20 they should be trained to seek God's kingdom first and trust that, in Him, all their needs will be met (Matthew 6:33). They should have confidence knowing that God's will for them is only good (Jeremiah 29:11). That no matter what happens, God is for them. He will work all things together for their good because they love Him and are called according to His purpose (Romans 8:28). And they need a solid understanding that transformation and the knowledge of God's will happens through the renewing of our minds (Romans 12:2).

I cannot stress the importance of cutting the parental cord enough during this stage. You have had your children for 20 years. You have sown good seed into their life. You have trained and taught, protected and prepared them to make good choices, be independent, and follow the Spirit's leading. It's time to let them go. Let God take the lead and trust Him to be faithful to His Word sown in their hearts.

In adulthood, our children should be ready to begin their own families: *"For this cause shall **a man** leave his father and mother and shall cleave unto his wife"* (Genesis 2:24, Mark 10:7). This man in Hebrew and Greek is an adult. Adults leave their parents and cleave to their spouses. They get married and sow righteous seeds to create another family who will know what it is to worship and honor God alone. But what about those that don't leave your house to marry, or don't marry until later in life? The parental cord of direct authority, oversight, and accountability must still be cut at adulthood, at 20.

Many parents wonder why their adult children avoid them or seem constantly frustrated with them. It might be because the parental cord has not truly been cut. They may fear being manipulated or treated like a child. They could fear your condemnation over their mistakes or your disappointment if they ask for advice then make a different decision. But in our new role as "friend," our children need to know that we trust them to make good decisions or deal with the consequences of their bad ones as an adult. Our children need to know that we are for them—no matter what. And that we will only give advice when it is asked of us. We must land the helicopter and trust God to guide our children through the next seasons of their lives.

Chapter 3 | GODLY SEED

Didn't the Lord make you one with your wife? In body and spirit you are his. And what does he want? Godly children from your union. So guard your heart; remain loyal to the wife of your youth.

Malachi 2:15, NLT

The most important function of the Christian parent is the raising and rearing of godly seed. This is one of the reasons we get married, as I mentioned in the last chapter. According to Malachi, God's plan for man to *"be fruitful and multiply"* was not just to *"replenish the earth"* (Genesis 1:28, KJV). God was not just looking for children; He wanted godly children—your children and mine.

It's been said that raising a child takes a village. But that is not true. It takes a dad and mom willing to take on the role of parenthood. I'm not saying no good can come from a single parent household. God's goodness and grace is amazing in all our failures and shortcomings (Romans 5:20). What I am saying is that God's best, His optimal plan, for our children is to experience the love and care of a father (a male) and a mother (a female). Our children's success and longevity are connected to knowing both. Fathers are important to a child's development. They speak truth to their children and reinforce their identity. Mothers are also important. They nurture their children and provide insight into their spiritual and emotional well-being that dads often miss.

Let's refer back to Ephesians 6: *"Children, obey your parents in the Lord, for this is right. Honor your father and mother, which is the first commandment with promise, that it may be well with you, and you may live long on the earth"* (vs. 1-3). Notice this commandment is for children, not adults. The right thing for children to do is obey their parents, not all adults. But today, society is trying to bypass parents. They want to remove children from their parent's protection. Schools are teaching things without parental knowledge or oversight. Doctors are advocating for treatment without parental consent, and in the name of gender care, removing parents' oversight and protection of their children. This is not right. God gave parents responsibility over their children, not school boards, doctors, or politicians.

I find it interesting that this commandment to children first appeared as part of the Ten Commandments in Exodus chapter 20 (vs. 12). Most people think of commandments as given to adults. But the New Covenant makes it clear that this command was given to children and given with a promise attached. If obeyed, children could be sure *"it would go well"* with them and they would *"live long on the earth."* In other words, if children learned to obey and honor their parents they would more easily learn to obey and honor other authorities in life—namely God, but also teachers, policemen, and their future employers—which leads to prosperity, success, and longevity in life. The Word does not say that life will be perfect or free of problems, but no matter what our children face, with this attitude of honoring God (learned first by honoring parents), they can prevail. Rebellion, Scripture tells us, is like the sin of witchcraft (I Samuel 15:23). It leads to unnecessary heartache and demonic assault. Obedience leads to long life.

When I worked with my children on honor and obedience I did so out of love for their well-being and concern for their futures. I never disciplined them in wrath or out of a selfish agenda. I didn't discipline them because I was embarrassed or hurt by their actions. All discipline—from birth to 20 years of age—should be rooted in the child's well-being, for if they learn to honor and obey you, their parents, they will more readily honor and obey God. That is what our discipline is preparing them for—relationship with God.

THE POWER OF PARENTHOOD

Recall the reason God chose Abraham: He would command his children to keep the way of the Lord (Genesis 18:19). Now consider Abraham's faith in the offering of Isaac. I believe Abraham knew the fullness of the gospel. He knew God's Son, the promised Seed, would have to die but that He would also rise again (Galatians 3:8, I Corinthians 15:1-4). Abraham knew Isaac was a miracle child, a type of Christ, and he saw the gospel at work through his obedience. Abraham realized that offering Isaac as a sacrifice was a type and shadow of what God would do with His Own Son, Jesus. Abraham had no thought of leaving his son dead on that mountain. He even told the servants who journeyed with him, *"Stay here with the donkey; the lad and I will go yonder and worship, and we will come back to you"* (Genesis 22:5). Abraham knew that if he obeyed God and offered Isaac, God would raise him from the dead.

Abraham's faith is amazing. But perhaps more amazing is Isaac's faith and obedience to his father! It was a three-day journey to Mount Moriah and Isaac had no idea what was in his father's heart; yet he obeyed. When they arrived at the mountain Isaac said, *"Look, the fire and the wood, but where is the lamb for a burnt offering?"* (Genesis 22:7). His father responded, *"My son, God will provide for Himself the lamb for a burnt offering"* (vs. 8). Which, of course, God did, but only after Abraham had built the altar, bound his son, and placed him upon it (vs. 13).

What son stands still while his father binds his hands? What son doesn't struggle or question when his father places him on top of an altar of sacrifice? And what son would stay on that altar as his father raised a knife to take his life? That is faith! And that is the picture of God's love and Jesus' obedience as the sacrificial lamb (Philippians 2:8).

Would your child obey like that? Or would you be chasing them around the mountain? Make no mistake, Abraham had diligently trained and taught Isaac, and the fruit of his labor was evident.

Now consider the life of David. King David was a great leader, but he was not a great father. He did not discipline his children, and it cost him (and them) dearly. One of his sons raped a sister (2 Samuel 13:1-21). Another killed his brother in revenge then plotted to overthrow his father's throne (2 Samuel 13:22-29, 15:1-12). Eli, the high priest in I Samuel was of a similar ilk. His sons, Hophni and Phineas, were wicked men who did not honor God or obey their father (I Samuel 2:12-17). Though they committed abominations in the temple, Eli refused to discipline them, and it did not end well for any of the family (vs. 22-25, 30-34). The Lord replaced them with *"a faithful priest who will serve me and do what I desire. I will establish his family, and they will be priests to my anointed kings forever"* (vs. 35, NLT).

Thank God for Abraham's obedience in raising a godly seed! May we learn from his example and be parents who work diligently to raise a righteous generation that fears the Lord.

Chapter 4 | TRAINING WITH THE ROD

The rod and reproof give wisdom: But a child left to himself bringeth his mother to shame.

Proverbs 29:15, KJV

When children are young, part of their training involves the *"rod of correction"* (Proverbs 22:15). The rod (also known as a spanking) is a temporary form of discipline used in the early childhood stage when children need a physical, concrete example that obedience brings life and blessing, and disobedience causes pain. In my experience, this mode of discipline is most effective between the ages of two to approximately ten. With my own children, it lasted until they were about eight.

Let me be clear. The *"rod of correction"* is not a rod of wrath. Once a child can reason and understand boundaries, consequences, and the principle of sowing and reaping other forms of discipline and chastening are just as effective. In fact, for most older children, when the consequence of their disobedience involves grounding or the loss of privileges (such as social media access), they would rather receive a spanking. In their mind, the spanking is less painful. It is quick and simple, whereas other forms of discipline can be extended for days. Regardless of the form of correction used, children should never be disciplined out of anger or frustration. All forms of discipline must stem from love, because *"The wrath of man worketh not the righteousness of God"* (James 1:20, KJV).

The purpose of correction—the rod and reproof—is wisdom. A child who does not understand why they are being disciplined will not grow in wisdom. It is up to parents to communicate, at an age-appropriate level, both what the child did wrong (disobeyed or did not honor) and how to make it right. Offering only the rod, the physical consequence, is not enough. Likewise, only reproving (lecturing) young children will not produce results. Children need both the rod and the reproof.

WHY THE ROD?

I think we all understand that misusing the rod (using it in anger, wielding it too hard or for too long, using it at too young or old of an age) is not healthy. But what is the purpose of the rod? The rod demonstrates the existence and purpose of boundaries. It uproots foolishness and provides consequences that are easily understood at every level. When used properly, the rod proves our love to our children and helps them learn to discern and resist temptation. The rod is a temporary form of discipline that protects parents from verbally abusing their children or cursing them with angry words. It gives children a concrete example of the pain self-centeredness brings, and it shows them the power of sowing and reaping.

BOUNDARIES

To be successful, children must learn early that life is governed by rules and boundaries. Everywhere they go in life, in every season, there will be rules—at school, on the job, in marriage, as a citizen. Just think of all the rules you have to abide by! Clocking in at work. Driving in traffic. Avoiding the "doghouse" at home. Paying taxes, registering a vehicle, checking out at the grocery store. Refusing to obey certain rules or submit to godly boundaries hurts ourselves and others and could even end in a residency in jail. (But guess what? In jail there are more boundaries. You eat what is set before you. You get up and go to bed at certain times. You work where they tell you to work and go where they tell you to go).

Not correcting our children hardens their heart to sin, and without the intervention of God's mercy and grace, will ultimately result in their rejection of Jesus. Rejecting Jesus will lead to a devil's hell, where guess what? There are still boundaries. Even Heaven has boundaries—just ask Satan and the fallen angels. Learning to recognize and live within boundaries leads to blessing. It protects us from harm.

FOOLISHNESS

Proverbs says, *"Foolishness is bound up in the heart of a child: The rod of correction will drive it far from him"* (vs. 22:15). Notice again it is the *"rod of correction,"* not the rod of wrath or anger. Many believe the rod was an instrument of Old Covenant wrath. They think it damages people. While the rod can harm others when used in wrath, so can verbal abuse, guilt, condemnation, and hollering. The rod was not part of the law. It was revealed in the book of wisdom. Under the law, rebellious children were stoned to death (Mark 7:10, Exodus 21:17, Leviticus 20:9). Spanking offers mercy to our children! Remove the rod and foolishness remains. So the rod of correction is not connected to the curses of the law; it is connected to the blessings of wisdom. We are not wiser than God. We must understand that foolishness, if not dealt with early in our children's lives, will harm them forever.

CONSEQUENCES

The rod gives our children consequences when the results of sowing and reaping are too far removed for a little one's understanding. Young children need immediate consequences. They can't reason cause and effect, sowing and reaping, action and reaction. The rod is how children learn personal responsibility. It's a form of hate not to teach our children that there are consequences to our actions.

We have an entire generation raised to believe all their problems are someone else's fault. Their lives are being destroyed because they won't own their mistakes and poor decisions. A child will never prosper if they don't learn to take responsibility for their own actions. The rod trains them early that disobedience causes pain.

In our home, the rod was called "Mr. Spoon." None of our children wanted to experience "Mr. Spoon" on their hind ends, but it taught them early the value of obedience and the consequence of disobedience. Many parents avoid the rod because they don't believe in hurting children. I don't believe in hurting children either, but the Bible is clear: *"Do not withhold correction from a child, for if you beat him with a rod, he will not die. You shall beat him with a rod, and deliver his soul from hell"* (Proverbs 23:13-14). The purpose of the rod is correction, not punishment. Not harm, wrath, or a release of anger. God's Word never implies we are to hurt our children. Instead, this temporary form of discipline serves to save them from the eternal consequence of sin.

In all discipline, parents must keep the end goal in mind. We are preparing our children for adulthood. An undisciplined child is unemployable. And that will hurt them. An undisciplined child is likely to wind up in divorce. And that will hurt both them and their families. An undisciplined child may go to prison. And that will hurt their future. But I can think of no greater hurt than a child who has no concept of personal accountability going to hell. That kind of hurt truly harms them. It lasts for eternity.

HATE VERSUS LOVE

Proverbs 13:24 tells us, *"He who spares his rod **hates** his son, but he who **loves** him disciplines him promptly."* As we have seen, withholding discipline from our children is a form of hate. They grow up unable to function in careers, marriage, or society.

They have no sense of boundaries, consequences, or personal responsibility which leads to a life of self-destruction. Discipline is not a feeling. It is a form of love. Most people think of hate and love as emotions rather than actions or inactions. But I John says, *"My little children, let us not love in word or in tongue, but in **deed** and in **truth**"* (vs. 3:18). Love is an action. Hate is an inaction. According to Scripture, parents who do not discipline their children are hating them.

RESISTING TEMPTATION

Young children have no concept of temptation. They don't know they are being selfish, nor do they understand the harm that causes. They can't discern Satan's devises. Thus a parent should not expect a three-year-old to resist the temptation to take their brother's toy when all the parent has done is warn them of the dangers of selfishness. They can't think in abstract concepts. They don't consider long-term effects. Their brains are not yet developed enough to understand, "If you continue operating in self-centeredness and pride, you won't have any friends in school. You won't be able to hold down a job.

You won't be able to function in marriage and family; you'll probably end up in divorce, paying alimony for the rest of your life. To cope, you'll abuse drugs and alcohol, become homeless, and resort to dumpster-diving for food. You could even end up in prison where someone will steal all of your stuff just like you stole your brother's toy. That will teach you for being selfish!" Children can't understand any of that. What they can understand is: "If you take your brother's toy again, we will have a meeting with Mr. Spoon."

You see, the proper use of the rod actually teaches children, in a concrete way, to resist the devil. Then, as adults, they will understand James 4:7 which says, *"Therefore submit to God. Resist the devil and he will flee from you."* The rod trains children early to deny self and the selfish behaviors that ruin our lives. It teaches them that pride leads to destruction and causes strife and contention (Proverbs 11:2, 13:10, 16:18).

TEMPORARY FORM OF DISCIPLINE

When we talk about the rod, we are talking about a short-term, time-tested form of discipline in which a flat-sided object (not the hand) strikes a child's gluteus maximus with precision. This "spanking" sends a signal to your child's brain that opens tear ducts and engages the synapses which fire a message to the child that says: "I'm not doing that again."

Again, let me be clear. I am not talking about beating a child in anger or wrath. A spanking is one to two swats delivered to their bottoms followed by instruction, hugs, and prayer. "Well doesn't that defeat the purpose?" you ask. Absolutely not. The purpose of a spanking isn't to guilt the child or punish them with your disapproval. Its purpose is to train them in boundaries. It is a consequence for disobedience; then we move on, providing our children with a biblical pattern of repentance and restoration. We hug them to show them we are not angry, nor are we going to hold anything over them. Instead we love them enough to bring correction and train them in the way they should go. We pray together as a way to show our kids that God is also involved in this process of growth.

Scripture is clear. God disciplines those He loves (Hebrews 12:6). He chastens and corrects all His legitimate children, but He does not do so in anger. While *"no chastening seems to be joyful for the present, but painful; nevertheless, afterward it yields the peaceable fruit of righteousness to those who have been trained by it"* (Hebrews 12:11). If God does this for us, why would we not discipline our children? Do we not want them to experience the *"peaceable fruit of righteousness?"* Do we not want to prepare them for the chastening of the Lord? The time they are with us—the time our children experience the physical rod of correction—is temporary. But it will yield great rewards that are eternal!

WORD CURSES OR GRACE

I know I have said this over and over, but it is the rod of correction parents wield, not the rod of anger (Proverbs 22:15). Too many parents don't understand the purpose of the rod, or they fear using it and harming their children. Yet they yell and threaten and cuss their kids. They get frustrated and call them names or slap them. These things are not okay. They are a result of man's anger and will not produce the righteousness of God (James 1:20). Only loving discipline can drive foolishness out of a child's heart.

Parents who reject the rod, calling it abusive, yet curse their children with harsh words are verbally abusing them. They say things like: "You never do anything right" or "You'll never amount to anything." They call them names and rewrite their identity when they say, "You're such a headache" or "You're nothing but a pain in my [you can fill in the blank]." These kinds of word curses are much more damaging than a spanking carried out in love. Parents who withhold correction and loving discipline from their children are not thinking of the eternal consequences of disobedience and rebellion (Proverbs 23:13-14).

Colossians 4:6 says, *"Let your speech always be with grace, seasoned with salt."* We are all called to be kind and forgiving to one another. That includes our children. The Word teaches, *"Let no corrupt word proceed out of your mouth, but what is good for necessary edification, that it may impart grace to the hearers. And do not grieve the Holy Spirit [...] Let all bitterness, wrath, anger, clamor, and evil speaking be put away from you [...] And be kind to one another tenderhearted, forgiving one another, even as God in Christ forgave you"* (Ephesians 4:29-32). We need to bless our children with our words, especially in discipline.

SELF-CENTEREDNESS

The rod of correction gives children a concrete example of the pain self-centeredness brings. Self-centeredness is pride. Pride leads to strife, conflict, failure, and destruction (Proverbs 13:10, 16:18). As Proverbs 13:10 says, *"Only by pride cometh contention: But with the well advised is wisdom."* Be "well-advised." Understand that any disobedience in your child is a result of pride in their heart. And according to God's wisdom, the rod will put a restraint on that selfishness and teach them to prefer others. It is an external form of denying self; one that, if learned early, will help them resist the destructive temptations of drugs, alcohol, and digital media.

I like to conduct the Walmart test to gauge where my children are on the "learning to deny self" scale. (The Walmart test is a rite of passage for every child and parent. But it doesn't have to happen at Walmart. Any store will do.) When your child wants something you were not already planning to buy, it is good to say, "Not now." This test helps them learn to harness their emotions and develop patience. And it teaches you the same thing—especially if they have a walleyed fit, fall on the floor and start foaming at the mouth while doing a 360. Just remember, this denying of self is a development process for both of you.

SOWING AND REAPING

Much of our lives rotate around the principle of sowing and reaping: *"Do not be deceived, God is not mocked; for whatever a man sows, that will he also reap. For he who sows to his flesh will of his flesh reap corruption, but he who sows to the Spirit will of the Spirit reap everlasting life"* (Galatians 6:7-8). When we sow to our flesh in thought or action, we reap corruption. Not from God, but from our flesh. Corruption is the process by which something goes from good to bad. We can all corrupt the good God wills for our lives by sowing bad seeds. But children can't comprehend that. It is too abstract. So the rod teaches them, on a small scale, how sowing and reaping works. "If I disobey, I will reap Mr. Spoon. So, I think I will choose to obey. Then I will reap a reward [even if that reward is simply the absence of pain]."

Unfortunately, many parents are deceived over the reality of sowing and reaping. They don't realize the harvest they are experiencing, even as it relates to their children's behavior, is a result of the seeds they have sown. Someone or something else is always to blame. Regardless, God is not mocked. His Word is true. Avoiding this principle and rejecting God's wisdom will only lead to corruption. After all, *"there is a way that seems right to a man, but its end is the way of death"* (Proverbs 14:12).

The philosophies of man spoil our lives (Colossians 2:8). They lead to pain and darkness, and ultimately societal collapse. While it is true that we reap some things in life we didn't sow to, most of the time, the pain in our lives is a direct result of the seeds we have sown. But thank God for His mercy! We can repent and experience crop failure on those bad seeds, and we can sow good seeds, believing for the harvest of righteousness in our lives. So discipline your children, for their sakes, and for the sake of our future. Consider God's wisdom and raise functional, disciplined children who will grow into fruitful, blessed adults.

Chapter 5 | PROVOKE NOT TO WRATH

And you, fathers, do not provoke your children unto wrath, but bring them up in the training and admonition of the Lord.

Ephesians 6:4

As with all things in life, parenthood requires balance. As parents, we are instructed to train our children (from zero to ten) and admonish or teach them (from ten to twenty) in the Lord. But in that training and teaching, we are also commanded not to provoke our children to wrath. Often, well-meaning parents mishandle discipline situations with their children in a desire for them to be and do all God has for them. If we are not careful to repent of those missteps, we can provoke our children to wrath. (Provoke means to anger, enrage, exasperate, or vex someone.) The most common things that provoke or exasperate children are anger and impatience, inconsistency, neglect, abuse, unclear expectations or consequences, humiliation, favoritism, harshness, and unreasonable punishments.

ANGER AND IMPATIENCE

"Like reproduces like," so we need to be careful how we approach our children. Anger and impatience from us will not bring out the best in them. The Scriptures instruct us, *"Let every man be swift to hear, slow to speak, slow to wrath; for the wrath of man does not produce the righteousness of God"* (James 1:19-20). Often, parents feel that no one listens unless they raise their voices or show anger. But the end never justifies the means. Scripture admonishes us to be quick to listen, slow to speak, and slow to become angry. As parents, we are our children's role models. Our discipline is preparing them for relationship with the Heavenly Father, so our chastening needs to model His. Remember, at 20, they will come out from under our covering and instruction and come under His. It is our job to prepare them for the way God disciplines and chastens. He never disciplines in wrath, impatience, condemnation, or guilt. I love the way the Passion

Translation relays this verse: *"Be quick to listen, but slow to speak. And be slow to become angry, for human anger is never a legitimate tool to promote God's righteous purpose."* Anger from you will reproduce anger in your child. Remember, godly discipline is about them and their future, not our feelings. When we are angry, we act out of bias and become unqualified to discipline. So, if emotions become heightened in any form of discipline, call for a timeout. Recuse yourself and pray before moving forward. You don't want to do or say something that will misrepresent God to your child.

INCONSISTENCY

When we discipline emotionally, we are inconsistent. If our children are only disciplined when we've had a bad day, and at all other times their bad behavior is ignored, we breed feelings of confusion and insecurity. Insecurity leads to fear, and fear destroys faith. Disobedience can't be wrong today but okay tomorrow, depending on our mood. Children need consistency. Without it, they will create consistency for themselves—even if that "consistency" is in the form of pushing your buttons until you erupt in anger.

NEGLECT

Scripture says, *"a child left to himself brings his mother to shame"* (Proverbs 29:15, KJV). We see the reality of this play out in culture every day. Children need boundaries. They need discipline in order to become productive and fruitful. Without it, children become hurt and angry. They feel abandoned and struggle to trust. These symptoms are especially prevalent in the adolescent stage. Listen parents, don't let your teenage children con you into believing they don't want you in their lives. They want and need your attention just as much now as they did during their younger years. And when they don't receive it in affirmations of love, they will demand it by acting out. So, when your children or grandchildren cry, "Watch this Papaw!" take the time to affirm your love and give them your attention.

ABUSE

2 Corinthians 10:8 tells us that all authority comes from God for the purpose of edification, not destruction. As parents, we cannot be abusive with any form of discipline. I once sent my children to their room with a, "Don't come out until you draw your first social security check." Too far? Of course! But we all laughed, and my method lost any similitude of discipline. Proverbs says, *"Like a roaring lion and a charging bear is a wicked ruler over the poor people. A ruler who lacks understanding is a great oppressor"* (vs. 28:15-16). We need understanding and self-awareness to be good parents, otherwise we end up oppressing our children instead of being their coaches and instructors in life. In all things, physical and verbal abuse is unacceptable for the Christian. Ephesians 4:29 says, *"Let no corrupt word proceed out of your mouth but what is good for necessary edification, that it may impart grace to the hearers."* Our words matter, so choose them wisely. Even in discipline, be gracious (Colossians 4:6). Don't put your children down or shut them down with wrong words. And if you do, apologize quickly.

UNCLEAR EXPECTATIONS AND CONSEQUENCES

It is not right or fair to discipline a child for something they don't know is wrong. If you have not given clear instructions, how can they be accountable to them? In all expectations, check for understanding. Did your child hear the rule or boundary given? Do they understand the consequences of disobedience? Without clarity in these things, we can provoke our children to wrath. For example, with adolescents: "Your curfew is at 10:00. What are the consequences if you're late? If you are late and these consequences are invoked, who's fault is that?" At this stage, we are not looking for blind obedience. We are teaching our children to process their actions, count the cost, and own their mistakes. Critical thinking is a part of preparing them for adulthood.

HUMILIATION

The goal of discipline is never to shame or embarrass our children, even if they embarrass us by throwing a fit at Walmart. That is just a parental rite of passage. It can be brutal, but don't give in to the temptation to cast the demon out of your child at the checkout line. Breathe. Count to ten, then deal with the issue in private. Don't humiliate your child. Be the adult. I Peter and Proverbs both say, *"Love covers the multitude of sin"* (1 Peter 4:8, Proverbs 10:12). That doesn't mean love excuses sin or tries to cover it up. But, like God, love doesn't expose or damage people publicly. I Corinthians 13 gives 16 character traits of love, what it looks and acts like. Verse five says love *"does not behave rudely, does not seek its own, is not provoked, thinks no evil."* And Romans 13:10 says, *"Love worketh no ill to his neighbor; therefore love is the fulfilling of the law"* (KJV). We represent God most fully when we love with His kind of love and do not work ill toward others.

FAVORITISM

God does not show favoritism, and neither should we. While I have been accused of having favorites, I am innocent. I can't help that my youngest daughter is nearly perfect! Even my oldest son agrees. She is his favorite, too. She really is special to us all, but favoritism can be a problem especially among blended families. Favoritism provokes children to wrath. Remember the story of Joseph and his brothers in Genesis 37? Jacob's favoritism toward Joseph was not wise. It provoked jealousy among the brothers, and they eventually conspired to sell Joseph into slavery. Genesis 37:4 says, *"But when his brothers saw that their father loved (Joseph) more than all his brothers, they hated him and could not say Peace (in friendly greeting) to him or speak peaceably to him"* (AMPC). While there is no excuse for what the brothers did, Jacob's obvious favoritism didn't help. In all families, favoritism needs to be watched for and dealt with quickly. This requires self-awareness on the part of the parents, and possibly some hard conversations between the two. There may be a blind spot in one of you that needs a second pair of eyes.

HARSHNESS

Being too hard or too strict with our children can discourage them. Many times, when we recognize a weakness of the flesh or respond to a child's failure, we react harshly. We forget that we are not only correcting and instructing them in righteousness, but also demonstrating God's grace and mercy. We must be gracious to our children in their mistakes so that we teach them to run to God, not from Him in their shortcomings. Be quick to forgive your children and extend mercy whenever possible. Doing so expresses grace (getting the good we don't deserve) and mercy (not getting the bad we do deserve) in ways they will never forget.

UNREASONABLE PUNISHMENT

To keep from exasperating our kids in punishment, the time must match the crime. Just like we don't invoke capital punishment, as a society, for shoplifting, so we, as parents, don't ground our teenagers for six months the first time they miss curfew. As children get older, we transition away from the physical rod and begin to create (and discuss) consequences that are just and fair. At times, every teen thinks any amount of discipline is unreasonable, but this too is a learning experience. Equity is one of the seven pillars in the house of wisdom, so we must learn to mete out just consequences without prejudice or partiality.

Chapter 6 | TEACHING

My people are destroyed for a lack of knowledge.

Hosea 4:6

The next phase of child development is teaching or preparation. This phase often overlaps a bit with the training phase because children are curious. They start asking questions early in life. It is important, as parents, to discern what level of information children are requesting in those early questions and have wisdom in answering them in an age-appropriate way. There will always be time during the teaching phase to answer them more fully. The teaching phase typically starts between the ages of eight to ten (depending on a child's maturity level and their capacity to process and apply information) and goes on through the teenage years. Teaching is a vital part of the preparation phase during which we equip our children for success in adulthood, marriage, and fulfilling the will of God for their lives. Hosea 4:6 tells us that, *"My people are destroyed for a lack of knowledge."* But Proverbs says, *"The mouth of the righteous is a well of life"* (vs. 10:11a). Parents need to be that well of life for their children during this phase and teach them the ways of the Lord. Without instruction in the ways of the Lord, they will perish.

I think a lot of parents understand that their children need knowledge during this time, but they often don't know what to teach them. There is so much to learn, it can feel overwhelming. When my children were younger, they asked a lot of questions. But sometime during their teenage years, the questions stopped. My wife and I had to initiate questions to stay engaged in their lives. We had to draw them out to understand what they were thinking and how they were processing experiences so we could learn what they needed to help them keep growing.

During the preparation phase, parents are helping their children discover their gifts and talents, their strengths and passions, and directing them toward their future careers. They are helping their children develop disciplines that will follow them the rest of their lives, things like a good work ethic, study habits, and self-awareness. They encourage teens in healthy esteem (especially their identification in Christ), making wise decisions, and healthy interpersonal relationships. All these things—the skills for today and a hope for the future—help children stand strong in the face of peer pressure and ungodly societal norms (culture).

One thing we have to remember and prepare our children for is that pressure never goes away. It doesn't end after high school or college like some people say or even hope. Peer pressure is something we all experience and have to learn to deal with throughout our lives. The earlier we learn to do that (i.e., while still under our father and mother's care) the more "natural" it will become to us. (I put the word natural in quotes, because this is really not a natural skill. It is a supernatural one—one that every believer is equipped with, but one that has to be exercised in order to see its fruit.) The three most common pressures we experience in life come from corrupt culture, developing sexuality, and the influence of friends.

1. CORRUPT CULTURE

Through our entire lives we are being subjected to a corrupt world endeavoring to conform us into an image other than Christ. Romans 12:2 starts out with, *"And do not be conformed to this world, but be transformed by the renewing of your mind."* Conformed means "to fashion alike," that is conform to the same pattern (Strongs-G4862 *suschematizo*). Dictionary.com defines conform as: "to act according to or be obedient to a rule or norm." There is cultural pressure to act in a way that violates God's ways and commandments. Like Proverbs says, *"There is a way that seems right to a man but its end is the way of death."* (vs. 14:12). Our children need to see us stand firm in the face of cultural pressure and not conform) to societal norms that violate Jesus and His kingdom principles. Our kids should see us live in the fear of God, not the fear of man. The fear of rejection if we do not look like, talk like, think like, or act like the world should not be what shapes our character. Our children need to see us conformed into the image of God's dear Son (Rom. 8:29).

Proverbs says that the fear of man brings a snare (vs. 29:25). It is a trap that kills our faith in God. John 5:44 says, *"How can you believe, who receive honor from one another, and do not seek the honor that comes from the only God?"* Caring more about what others think or say than what God thinks or says kills faith. We must teach our children to process and overcome this type of pressure early in life so that their faith-obedience to God is not compromised. Giving in to the fear of man—whether through societal pressure in the media or on the job, voices of politicians, political correctness, college professors or woke activists—will intimidate our children and push them into unrighteousness. Many godly parents panic when their children or teenagers have a faith crisis. But this is a good thing. If their faith is tested early (while still under your covering), you can help them process it properly. Then their faith has an opportunity to develop into a godly fear of the Lord. They will be able to stand for truth and righteousness instead of following the crowd of culture off a cliff. A faith crisis in adulthood has far greater repercussions than one in their teenage years.

2. SEXUAL PRESSURE

During adolescence, bodies are changing, and hormones are raging. Sexual curiosity is normal. But at times the pressure to engage in premarital sex can feel overwhelming. As uncomfortable as it may be, teaching a biblical perspective of sexuality is vital during this time. We must share with our children the dangers of sex before marriage, but also—and this is not something the Church has done a good job of—we must also teach them the beauty and pleasure God intended for sexual intimacy within the marriage covenant. If, as parents, we don't teach them, their friends and the world will. Hebrews 13:4 says, *"Marriage is honorable among all, and the bed undefiled; but fornicators and adulterers God will judge."* This scripture covers both the blessing of sexual intimacy within the bounds of marriage and God's judgment on sexual immorality. I Corinthians 6:18 says, *"Flee sexual immorality. Every sin that a man does is outside the body, but he who commits sexual immorality sins against his own body."* All sin has a wage, but the wages of sexual sin come into the body (Romans 6:23). One of those consequences is venereal disease. HIV is still a part of our world, and it is not the only consequence of sex outside marriage. But within marriage, God sanctifies our sexual activities and deems them wholesome and pleasurable. In other words, sex is amoral. Within God's boundaries it is good; outside, it is bad. When I was teaching my children about sex, I tried to help them understand this concept using the natural examples of water and fire. Both water and fire are amoral. They are neither good nor evil. You can't live three days without water, yet you can't live three minutes underneath it. Water within the bounds of a riverbank is a blessing. Outside those bounds, we call it a flood. It creates destruction. Likewise, in the boundaries of a fireplace, fire is a blessing. It provides warmth to the whole house. Outside that boundary, fire threatens all who live in (and out) of the home. If not contained, fire can burn down an entire city. We can see this principle demonstrated throughout Scripture, so take the time to teach it to your children. I will be covering the subject of the pleasures of sexuality within marriage and perils outside of marriage in detail in an upcoming book about raising teenagers.

3. FRIENDS

I Corinthians 15:33 is clear, the company we keep plays a huge role in the trajectory of our lives: *"Do not be deceived. Evil company corrupts good habits."* Yet many are deceived about this. Parents expect their children to overcome the bad influence of their friends when, as adults, they struggle to stand firm in the face of peer pressure. How many adults cave in the workplace when their company celebrates pride month or when a coworker tells an inappropriate joke? We need to be more like the three Hebrew children who did not bow to societal pressure and turned the king's heart with their commitment to God (Daniel 3). How did they do this? One of the ways was the encouragement of their friends. They had each other. This is why it is so important that we continue to assemble as the Body of Christ (Hebrews 10:25). We need each other. We need good, mature, loyal-to-Jesus friends who can encourage us to stand strong and hold us accountable when we face temptation. Proverbs 13:20 says, *"He who walks with wise men will be wise. But the companion of fools will be destroyed."* As parents, we need to know who our children are spending time with and where they are at all times. We also need to teach them how to choose godly friends. They will likely push the boundaries on this, and that's okay. But do not disengage. Kids need someone to help them make the hard decisions, and that someone is you. You are not their friend right now. I'm not saying you can't have fun with your kids or that you should be anything other than kind and loving. But you are not their buddy or pal. (That comes in the adult stage.) You are their guardian, their protector and life coach. You have to teach your children to love others without participating in bad behaviors. You have to teach them the doctrine of separation (2 Corinthians 6:14-18). Teach them to love the local drug dealer but not hang out with them, to love the addict but not be friends. Children have to learn that there are certain people they need to avoid. Romans 16:17 says, *"Note those who cause divisions and offenses, contrary to the doctrine which you learned, and avoid them."* Our kids need to learn early to avoid drama. They need friends that draw them closer to Christ, not away from Him.

TIPS FOR THE TEENAGE YEARS

The key during these years is relationship. Help your children learn to build healthy relationships both in and out of the home. But don't forget to practice what you preach. Be a good example and role model in this area. And have fun together. Here are a few things Sue and I did to keep our family growing together during these years.

- We made our home the hangout place. When our kids were at home, we knew they were safe and having fun with their friends. We also got to know their friends and could see if and when we needed to redirect them in the choosing/maintaining of healthy relationships.

- We taught our children that as long as they were having a positive impact on their friends, they could remain friends. Whenever a friend began having a negative impact on our child, we helped them see they had moved into an unhealthy relationship.

- We had the local pizza place on speed dial.

- We stocked up on good movies and popcorn.

- We planned fun family nights.
- We sometimes took our kid's friends with us on mini vacations.

One thing we didn't have to do with our kids but have had to do with our grandchildren is to supervise their digital space. It's important to teach kids that no digital space is private—not only in your home as you strive to protect them, but also in the world. Things posted on social media today can be used against them tomorrow. Their brains are not fully developed. They don't always know when they are veering off into dangerous territory. Digital addiction is real, so limit the amount of time your children spend on tech/media platforms. I Corinthians 6:12 tells us that while everything is permissible, not everything is beneficial: *"Even though I am allowed to do anything, I must not become a slave to anything"* (NLT). Inappropriate images, text messages, and comments can damage their developing brains and affect them for years to come.

Teach your children to make good friends (and wise decisions) during this season. Proverbs 18:24 (KJV) tells us, *"A man that hath friends must shew himself friendly and there is a friend that sticks closer than a brother."* And in those awkward times of struggles with friendships, remind them that Jesus is our friend that sticks closer than a brother. Encourage them to keep treating people the way they wish to be treated, not the way they are treated (Luke 6:31). Don't retaliate when things go wrong. Don't double down to force someone's apology. Teach them to recognize that we can't control other's actions. We can only control our own. Remember God's commandment to *"Love your neighbor as yourself"* (Leviticus 19:18 / Matthew 19:19). And hold tight to the truth that no matter what man does or doesn't do, says or doesn't say, they have a choice to *"Let God be true and every man a liar"* (Romans 3:3-4). Their friend's behavior does not nullify God's faithfulness nor does it change who they are or how they should respond.

Chapter 7 | FOUNDATIONS BY ADULTHOOD

So this is what the Lord God says: "See, I lay a stone in Zion, a tested stone, a precious cornerstone, a sure foundation; the one who believes will never be shaken.

Isaiah 28:16, Berean Standard

Remember Jesus' story of the wise and foolish builders (Matthew 7:24-27)? One man built his house on sand, the other on rock. Though both houses experienced similar severe weather, one fell while the other stayed standing. The difference? Their foundations. The same is true in our lives. Without a solid foundation, we will not survive the storms of life. Our children need those foundations as well, and it is our job, as parents, to provide for them. Our children should not leave home without a basic understanding of who God is, who they are in Christ, and what they have been called to do (and be) in partnership with Him. But if we don't have these basic foundations laid by the time they are 20, it may be too late. It certainly is more difficult to try to build our house in the storm versus laying our foundation for the storm.

BASICS NO CHILD SHOULD LEAVE HOME WITHOUT

At 20, our children are adults. They are responsible and held accountable to God for their actions. They have been through the training and teaching phases with us, and now, it is time to transition into adulthood. This can be hard for parents; typically, because they've mixed up the order of stages. They tried to be their children's friend too early (instead of parents) and now don't know if their children are ready to leave the nest. But by adulthood, whether we are ready for it or not, we must transition from relating to our children as Parent to being their friend and life coach. We only give advice when our children ask for it, and we recognize their right to accept or reject that advice without censure. Our children do not dishonor us if they choose differently than we would or if they feel God leading another way. We are not accountable to God for their life choices.

But no child should leave home without these basic understandings:

GOD LOVES YOU

All have sinned and need a Savior, yet God loves you. God's love was manifested on the cross when Jesus died for our sins and rose again for our justification. Our children must understand the importance of turning from sin and confessing Jesus as Lord of their life, without it, all else is forfeited (Romans 10:8-10). They need to know that God's kind of love is unconditional, unmerited, and intentional. There is nothing they can do good to get Him to love them more, nor is there anything they can do bad enough to have Him love them less. This knowledge will cause their faith to work (Galatians 5:6). It will cast out fear and allow them to run boldly to Him in their time of need (I John 4:18, Hebrews 4:16).

GOD IS FOR YOU

God is good. He has good plans for our children—plans to prosper them, not to harm them, plans for their future success (Jeremiah 29:11). No matter what happens in life, God is for them, not against them (Romans 8:31). He does not punish us as our sins deserve (Psalm 103:10, Galatians 3:13, Romans 8:1-4). Even in discipline, He desires only our good (Hebrews 12:5-6). He is faithful. We cannot be too redundant in teaching our kids these things.

THE FEAR OF THE LORD

A healthy, wholesome fear of the Lord is not tormenting. It is not a fear of wrath or rejection (I Timothy 1:5, I John 4:16-18). Fear of God involves worship. It is a reverence for who He is as Creator God (Job 1:20, Matthew 4:10, Deuteronomy 6:13). Jesus operated in this kind of fear, and so must we (Isaiah 11:2). A wholesome fear of God is the beginning of wisdom and knowledge (Proverbs 1:7, 2:5). It is to be awestruck by His power, goodness, faithfulness, and mercy. To fear the Lord is to hate evil (Proverbs 8:13). Proverbs says the fear of the Lord prolongs our days on the earth (vs. 10:27). It gives us confidence and provides us with refuge (Proverbs 14:26-27). And Job says, *"Behold, the fear of the Lord, that is wisdom, and to depart from evil is understanding*" (vs. 28:28). Who doesn't want those promises for their children?

AUTHORITY OF SCRIPTURE

Our children also need to know that God's Word is final authority. It is unbiased truth that endures forever (Matthew 24:35). The Word of God sanctifies us (John 17:17). It sets us free and gives us direction in life (John 8:31-32, Psalm 119:105). The Word delivers us from destruction and brings healing (Psalm 107:20).

Mine and Sue's children learned their ABCs with scripture. In preschool, their teacher taught them that:

A – **A**ll have sinned and come short of the glory of God. (Romans 3:23)

B – **B**elieve on the Lord Jesus Christ and thou shalt be saved. (Acts 16:31)

C – **C**hildren obey your parents in the Lord for this is right. (Ephesians 6:1)

This continued all the way through the letter Z. Our children still remember those truths and are teaching them to our grandchildren! I remember a time when our oldest daughter was about six. We were out to eat with a pastor and his leaders, one of whom asked our daughter what she was learning in school. She stood up and quoted the alphabet with Scripture references, from A to Z. The table was so impressed they (and other eavesdropping patrons in the restaurant) clapped for her accomplishment. Her face was beaming! Her mom and I were pretty proud, too!

Never underestimate the power of God's Word in a sensitive heart. The seed planted there will produce a harvest (I Corinthians 3:6).

A HEALTHY ESTEEM

Every child should know their value—both to God and their parents—before leaving home. I'm not promoting a healthy self-esteem in the sense of pride or arrogance in oneself. But neither am I advocating for a negative self-image. Self is the root of pride, and pride is the impetus of sin. But God doesn't want us living in low self-esteem either. He doesn't want us living in self at all. We are worth more to Him than that (Romans 5:8). God has called us to a high Christ-esteem. A healthy esteem is seeing oneself united to Christ. In Christ we have a positive Christ image, not self-image. In Christ we discover our new creation life and God's workmanship in us. Our kids need to know who they are in Christ is beautiful and precious in the eyes of God.

We need to protect our children from attacks on their identities, not necessarily by removing them from the world, but by teaching them their new identity in Christ. A positive Christ-image helps us deny self, take up our cross, and follow Jesus (Matthew 16:24).

Before our children leave home, they need to know who they are in Christ and be able to separate their identity from their performance so they can keep growing in their knowing of what it means to be God's child.

A GOOD WORK ETHIC

By 20, our children need to know how to work and provide for themselves (2 Thessalonians 3:6-

12). Work is part of God's image in man. In the beginning, God worked six days, and on the seventh, He rested (Genesis 2:2). We follow the pattern He set by working and resting as well. In the Garden, the first thing God gave Adam was a job (Genesis 2:19). Working is part of our worship to God (Colossians 3:17). It's how we have resources so that we can give (Ephesians 4:28). Mankind is less than human when he can work yet doesn't work. The value of work in contributing to our personhood and esteem is truly amazing. It is literally our worship of God. Scripture teaches that the work we do isn't to be seen of men, but it is an offering to God (Colossians 3:23, Ephesians 6:6-8). Our children must learn to earn their own way through work. Paul instructs the early church that, *"Those who are such* **[lazy busybodies]** *we command and exhort through our Lord Jesus Christ that they work in quietness and eat their own bread"* (2 Thessalonians 3:12). Work contributes to our healthy esteem. It provides for us and future families and blesses the larger community. A civil, functional society depends on each generation having a good work ethic and passing that value on to their children.

FINANCIAL STEWARDSHIP

Finances are not just carnal. They are spiritual. Children need to know that learning to handle natural things prepares them to handle spiritual things. Jesus taught that, *"He who is faithful in what is least* **[finances]** *is faithful also in much; and he who is unjust in what is least is unjust also in much"* (Luke 16:10, brackets added). We must teach our children to honor the Lord in everything by training them to give *"the first fruits"* of their labors to the Lord. When they do that, God blesses their storehouses and investments (Proverbs 3:9-10).

Before our children leave home, they need to know what God says about giving, tithing, sowing, saving, and preparing storehouses. And they need opportunities to practice what His Word says. They need to understand that biblical prosperity is a partnership. God promises to provide, but we, in faith, partner with Him in stewardship. Get money into your child's hands early. They can earn money with chores or special projects. Be creative and start teaching them how to handle finances. Teach them how to honor God with their money and use it to meet different needs.

One of my children, before they had a job and access to their own money, asked if they could give a pair of their shoes to someone at school who needed them. Absolutely! I broke out in a happy dance that day. My child was learning to conquer covetousness. Covetousness is idolatry (Colossians 3:5). But giving breaks its foothold. Teaching children to deny self, pray and believe, save their money, and work toward their goals are important life skills. It makes them master over their money instead of allowing money to master them (Matthew 6:22-24). And when they see God's faithfulness, their faith will grow. Thanksgiving will well up in their hearts and further guard them from idolatry.

REPENT AND FORGIVE

Everyone needs to know how to forgive. And everyone needs to know how to humble themselves and repent. Repentance is the road to transformation. It's what mind renewal is all about—a change of mind and direction (Romans

12:2). Unforgiveness and offense are two of Satan's biggest weapons. So let's not be ignorant of his devises (2 Corinthians 2:11). Learn to say, "I'm sorry," and learn to forgive whether or not you hear the apology you want. Don't let bitterness defile you or your children (Hebrews 12:15). Teach them to repent quickly when they mess up and forgive others when they are wronged (Matthew 6:12).

PREPARATION FOR THE MARRIAGE ALTAR

Two of the biggest decisions we make in life are submitting to Jesus as Lord and choosing who to marry. We've already talked about the importance of introducing your children to Christ early in life and teaching them to grow and develop in His Word and the leading of the Holy Spirit. This training in hearing His voice and walking by faith will help them when they make the decision of who to marry. They won't base that decision solely on their feelings or what they see with their physical eyes.

During their adolescent years, get your children involved in supervised group activities with people of the opposite sex. Things like youth group, youth camp, and conferences can rub some of the rough edges off their communication and social skills. Invite groups of teens to your house for game nights, backyard BBQs, and movie nights. Monitor how they relate to their peers, and in private times, teach them the skills they are missing. The teen years are awkward, but that is just a part of the learning process. (I will devote a whole chapter on this in my upcoming book on raising teenagers).

PRAYER

No one inherently knows how to pray. We have to be taught. John taught his disciples to pray. Jesus taught His (Luke 11:1-4). And we need to teach our children to pray. Children learn by example. They also learn through direct teaching. In prayer, they need both.

Pray with your children. Pray over them. Bless them and let them hear you. (I have several free resources to help you with this; you can find them on my website or by calling our helpline. Ask for "Blessing Your Children" and "The Fundamentals of Prayer.") Leverage special moments to teach prayer: Bedtime, mealtime, before tests or school presentations, after they've been hurt, etc. And teach them the model prayer that Jesus used to teach His disciples to pray: *"Our Father in heaven, hallowed be Your name. Your kingdom come. Your will be done on earth as it is in heaven. Give us this day our daily bread. And forgive us our debts, as we forgive our debtors. And do not lead us into temptation, but deliver us from the evil one. For Yours is the kingdom and the power and the glory forever. Amen"* (Matthew 6:9-13). Keep it simple and short. But engage with them in prayer in their everyday lives and show them how relevant faith can be.

Chapter 8 | DIFFERENT KINDS OF LOVE

Let love be without hypocrisy. Abhor what is evil. Cling to what is good.

Romans 12:9

So much confusion exists in our culture over love. We use the word to express so many emotions, that it has become descriptive of nothing. We say: "I love ice cream!" "I love the Dallas Cowboys!" "I love my dog." "I love my wife." Whether you've used those expressions or not, I pray there is a difference between the love you have for your dog and that of your wife. (And it better not be more love for your dog!) Love is vital to our development and our relationships. It's part of our common language. But are you prepared to answer the question, "How do I know when I'm in love?" Most parents are not. They tend to answer with "Well, uh… you'll just know." Two weeks later, when their child comes back saying, "I'm in love" they immediately know their child has fallen into infatuation, not love. But they still aren't prepared to respond to the "But you told me I'd know!" During the teaching phase of childrearing, one of the most important concepts we can instill in our children is the meaning of love.

God created every one of us to love and be loved, but our children need to know what love looks like so they can learn to recognize it in their own lives and actions and in the actions of others (I Corinthians 13:4-8, Titus 2:4, I Thessalonians 4:9). In Jesus' day the Greeks and philosophers used at least seven different words to describe love. They are:

1. AGAPE

The selfless love of God. Agape is Who God is. It is the highest form of love, the type of love God has for us, wills to reproduce in us, and works through us (Romans 5:5-8, I John 4:19). Agape is an unconditional, unmerited love. It is based on God's character and actions, not our conduct or emotions. Agape doesn't depend on any other type of love. It can be expressed to God, one another, or even strangers. Agape is connected to the concept of altruism and in the King James Version of Scripture is translated as charity. Agape is the practice of unselfish concern for another. It is the foundation for the other kinds of love and gives longevity to each. Agape is what causes us to reach our full potential.

2. PHILIA

This is an affectionate, friendship love. Sometimes people call it "brotherly love." Philia is an emotional bond characterized by loyalty and trust. It can be shared among friends or family members. Philia is encouraging, kind, and thoughtful. It is a platonic, yet meaningful love; something that is purely spiritual and wholesome, completely free from sensual desire. I Samuel 18 talks about this special kind of love in the friendship between Jonathan and David: *"The soul of Jonathan was knit with the soul of David and that Jonathan loved him as his own soul"* (vs. 1, KJV). In philia, we truly value others. We cheer others on toward success and prosperity without envy or jealousy. In philia, people often share common interests and simply enjoy being in one another's company.

3. EROS

A romantic, passionate, physical love that expresses itself through sexuality. This type of love was named after the Greek god of love, Eros. (In Rome, his name was Cupid.) According to myth, his golden arrows were responsible for making people "fall in love." They were struck with uncontrollable feelings of physical attraction, passion, and lust. Basically, Eros made lovers victims. They could fall into and out of this type of love as easily and unpredictably as a bee taking flight. Scripture, however, says eros needs boundaries. It is dangerous when exercised outside them. Though Hollywood makes billions on exalting this kind of love, long-lasting relationships are not built on eros. It is a part of, and reserved for, marriage, but it is not the foundation (Hebrews 13:4, I Corinthians 7:2-5). The best form of eros is built on the foundation of philia. That's what makes it sustainable.

4. STORGE

Familial love. This is the unconditional love of a father and mother for their children. Storge is protective and nurturing. It is one-sided (even if a child reciprocates love) and benevolent; it expects nothing in return. Storge sees and meets the needs of another, protects the other, and remains faithful to them no matter what..

5. PHILAUTIA

Self-love. This kind of love must be kept in balance. It can be healthy when surrendered to Christ, but it easily becomes narcissistic when left to itself. Philautia is self-care. Think about the last time you flew on a plane. When the flight attendants go over safety procedures, what do they say about the oxygen mask? Put on your own mask before assisting another, even a child. That feels wrong, but we can't give what we don't have. We have to take care of ourselves to be a blessing to others (Matthew 22:39). There is a healthy self-love that grows when we see ourselves in Christ (the healthy Christ esteem we explained in the previous chapter).

Remember we are to love our neighbor as **ourselves**.

6. LUDUS

Playful, flirtatious love. Ludus is that feeling of care-free attraction that comes with infatuation. It is a shallow, zero commitment type of love that can easily lead to no good. In Latin, ludus means to play, as in a game. If left unchecked it often devolves into seduction and "casual sex." But there is nothing casual about sex.

7. PRAGMA

Committed, long-lasting love. Pragma is the opposite of ludus. It is an enduring, "tough it out" sort of love that thinks long-term. Pragma is about commitment, companionship, and dreams of the future. It is often an extension of agape love in the home and holds the mindset of *"through patience and sacrifice we can make it work together."* Our English word "pragmatic" derives from this word for love. Pragma causes us to ask: What is the practical consideration in our dilemma? What is the right thing to do?

As you can see, the English word love is a complex idea. But none of these loves are meant to be exclusive of one another. They all work together, with agape as the foundation, in healthy, Christ-centered lifestyles.

Agape love is not of this world. It does not come from the flesh, nor does it depend on our feelings. But it does affect our feelings in a positive, productive way. God's kind of love has to be taught (I Thessalonians 4:9, Titus 2:4). It is not something that falls from the sky or rides on the tip of an arrow. Love grows as we grow in relationship with the Lord.

Source:

"8 Greek Words For Love That Will Make Your Heart Soar." Dictionary.com, 28 Mar. 2024, www.dictionary.com/e/greek-words-for-love/.

Chapter 9 | GOD'S KIND OF LOVE

This is how we know what love is: Jesus Christ laid down his life for us. And we ought to lay down our lives for our brothers and sisters.

I John 3:16, NIV

By the time children reach adulthood, they need to understand God's kind of love. Without it, they will be deceived. For what the world calls love is really perversion and lust. Yet many immature Christians embrace whatever the world presents as love even when those things are abominations in the eyes of God. The world speaks of love with no love of God in their hearts. They don't understand His kind of love so how can they give it?

The entire message of the Bible is summed up in this: Love God and love your neighbor as yourself. But if we don't love God first, we cannot love people with His kind of love. During Jesus' ministry someone asked, *"Teacher, which is the great commandment in the law?" Jesus said to him, "'You shall love the LORD your God with all your heart, with all your soul, and with all your mind.' This is the first and great commandment. And the second is like it: 'You shall love your neighbor as yourself.' On these two commandments hang all the Law and the Prophets"* (Matthew 22:35-40). By the time our children reach 20, our goal should be for them to love God and esteem others, including their siblings and future spouse. What does that look like? According to Romans *"love does no harm to a neighbor"* (vs. 13:8-10). That doesn't mean love won't speak up when it sees evil. Jesus was God made flesh, and though He didn't condemn us over sin, neither did He condone or celebrate it. He warned us of the wrath to come and gave us a way out (Matthew 11:20-24, John 8:11, John 5:14). I Corinthians 13 says that God's kind of love does not rejoice in iniquity; rather it rejoices in truth (vs.6). So let's look at some truths about God's love.

1. God's love is taught not caught. Paul wrote, *"But we don't need to write to you about the importance of loving each other, for God himself has taught you to love one another"* (I Thessalonians 4:9, NLT). God teaches us to love through His Word and Spirit. The world views love as a romantic, euphoric feeling. But God loves with action and in truth (I John 3:18). What is truth? God's Word (John 17:17, 8:31-32). So if we want to love like God, we must treat one another as directed in His Word.

2. Love is of God, not of this world. Love is not of us or our emotions. John wrote, *"Beloved let us love one another, for **love is of God**; and everyone who loves is born of God and knows God. He who does not love does not know God, for **God is love.**"* (1 John 4:7-8). Human beings cannot love independent of God. Any "love" we see outside relationship with and knowledge of God is not God's kind of love. It is a poor imitation at best. To love with God's kind of love, we have to know Him and be born of Him. This is why Scripture teaches us to marry other believers (2 Corinthians 6:14). To marry outside the community of faith is to go into fulltime missionary work. A lost spouse cannot love with God's kind of love. It's not in them.

3. God is love. Again, I John 4:8 says, *"He who does not love does not know God, for **God is love.**"* A world that does not know God cannot tell your children what love is. When the world says, "love is…" or "love wins," they leave God out of their definitions and reasonings. Love is the very nature of who God is and cannot be known independent of God Himself. God is holy, and calling love something unholy is a deception or perversion. Notice, "God is love" not just has love. God doesn't just have love for you and your children—He is it! If you <u>have</u> something it can be measured, and it has limitations and boundaries; but if you <u>are</u> something, then it just is. If you have water, you can have 16 ounces, 5 gallons, or a pool full of it. It can be said that you have more or less water. But if you are H_2O then you are the same to everyone. God doesn't have more love for others and less love for you or vice versa. He loves us all the same because it is who He is. You cannot do enough good to get Him to love you more or enough bad for Him to love you less. He loves you and your children with the same exact love He has for Jesus. Jesus is praying in John 17 for His disciples and for us who believe on Him through their testimony. He is praying for our unity and in verse 23 He says: *"I in them and you in Me; that they may be made perfect in one, and that the world may know that You have sent Me, and have loved them as You have loved Me."* WOW! God loves us with the same love He has for Jesus! How? Because He is love!

4. Love is revealed in the cross. I John 4:9-10 says, *"God showed how much he loved us by sending his one and only Son into the world so that we might have eternal life through him. This is real love—not that we loved God, but that he loved us and sent his Son as a sacrifice to take away our sins"* (NLT). Jesus' sacrifice, while we were still sinners, was a demonstration of God's love (Romans 5:8). He loved us when we didn't deserve it, and He continues to love us though we could never earn it. God's love never runs out (Jeremiah 31:3). We know God loves us by the cross, not our feelings or circumstances.

5. God's love is perceived. It is known by revelation. We do not always feel God's love. But we can always see it in His acts of kindness and compassion, most especially through His sacrifice on the cross(I John 3:16, KJV). In our culture, we have reduced love to an uncontrollable emotion—something that just happens, like a virus. But God's love is not like that. His love is a choice demonstrated in words and actions that others can perceive.

6. Love sees a need and supplies it. When Abraham arrived at Mt. Moriah to offer Isaac in obedience to God, Isaac asked where the sacrifice was. Abraham replied, *"God will provide for Himself the lamb for a burnt offering."* (Genesis 22:8). And later, *"then Abraham lifted his eyes and looked, and there behind him was a ram caught in a thicket by its horns."* (vs. 13). God's faithful love led Abraham to call that place *"Jehovah Jireh / The-Lord-Will-Provide"* (vs. 14 KJV/NKJV). God sees and God provides because of His love. In parenthood, love sees and provides for the physical, emotional, intellectual, and spiritual needs of our children; and love teaches our children to perceive and meet the needs of others.

7. God's love sacrifices. It serves. As Jesus' earthly ministry was ending, He was celebrating Passover with His disciples. John says that Jesus, knowing Judas (His betrayer) was sitting at the table with Him, rose up, laid aside His garments, and began to wash His disciples' feet (John 13). John

13:1 says, *"When Jesus knew that His hour had come…having loved His own who were in the world, He loved them to the end."* Jesus also knew Peter would deny Him. He knew the others would forsake Him. Yet "He loved them to the end." What amazing love! This is the kind of love God has called each of us to have for our children, and to teach our children to have for their families. There is no such thing as family independent of sacrificial love. We sacrifice time, money, food, preferences. Sacrifice upon sacrifice. I see people all the time making decisions to uproot their families, take their kids out of good schools or their families away from a good church, to move across country for an additional five or six thousand dollars a year. That is not love. Love makes itself available. It puts other's needs above its own and is loyal to the end. We have to learn to sacrifice things for the good of our homes, or we will sacrifice our homes for more things.

8. God's love is steadfast and unconditional. It is based on God's character, not our conduct. God loved us when we were His enemies, and He proved that love in the gift of His Son (Romans 5:8-10).

Now who (or what) can separate us from that love? Can hardship? Threats? Persecution? Lack? Danger? Pain or war? No! In all these things, His love helps us overcome (Romans 8:35-37). As Paul writes, *"For I am persuaded that neither death nor life, nor angels nor principalities nor powers, nor things present nor things to come, nor height nor depth, nor any other created thing, shall be able to separate us from the love of God which is in Christ Jesus our Lord"* (Romans 8:38-39). While we never condone sin in another, loving them with God's kind of love means we also do not allow it to separate us from them. In a world where love is hypocritical and selfish, our love must be a shining example of the love of God. It must remain steadfast.

9. God's love accepts us where we are but never gives up on our ability to change. People hurt us, sometimes intentionally. But God's love sustains us, and God's love in us helps us to separate what that person did with who they are. It allows us to keep loving, even in the hurt, and believe in their ability to learn and grow. When we excel in love like this, even in correction, we express who God is and give the other person a chance to know Him.

10. God's love forgives. The purpose of God sending His Son was forgiveness and reconciliation (John 3:16-17). That is the heart of love—relationship. Never be too proud to ask for forgiveness, and do not withhold forgiveness from anyone else. As believers, we should always work toward reconciliation. That doesn't mean we put ourselves back into dangerous situations, but we leave the door open for God's grace to work. Ephesians 4:32 says, *"And be kind to one another, tenderhearted, forgiving one another, even as God in Christ forgave you."* . While we can't force others to reconcile, we can keep our heart right toward them. We can forgive, own our mistakes, and leave the door open for God to work in both party's lives.

THE POWER OF FORGIVENESS

Not only does God's love empower us to forgive, but it also enables us to fess up when we mess up knowing that our mistake will not change God's acceptance of us as His children. And when we ask someone, especially a child or family member, to forgive us, we express that truth to them as well.

Apologizing recognizes the inherent value and dignity of others. Saying "I'm sorry, please forgive me," highlights how you value someone. It models humility and grants the wronged person respect. It is impossible to go through this life, your marriage, or parenthood without making mistakes. We all know that, but too often pride prevents us from verbalizing it. Yet Scripture says humility is the number one ingredient for a successful life: *"Yes, all of you be submissive to one another, and be clothed with humility, for 'God resists the proud, but gives grace to the humble.' Therefore humble yourselves under the mighty hand of God, that He may exalt you in due time,"* (I Peter 5:5-6).

When we humble ourselves and reveal our need for mercy, we simultaneously reveal another's need to forgive. Our kids must learn how to forgive so that they can be free from the prison of anger. There is an underlying anger in the hearts and minds of this generation that concerns me. It is hidden, under the radar. But it occasionally boils over in assaults and school shootings. I believe we're actually getting to the point where we could see a revolution, an internal war, in this country. We need to teach our children to be quick to forgive. And we need to model how to do that to others.

Asking for forgiveness cuts off anger, resentment, and bitterness before it can defile like a cancer. When we model and ask for forgiveness, we deliver those we've hurt from torment. I remember coming home one time and seeing my son's pigsty of a room. I don't remember how old he was, but I know his mom had instructed him to clean up and he had not obeyed. I raised my voice. I don't remember what I said, but it was something like, "Obey your mother and get this room cleaned up! Do it NOW." It scared him. I had never raised my voice before, and I shouldn't have then, but I'd had a bad day and was venting my frustration. When I walked out of the room Sue told me I needed to go back. I turned around and saw my son crying.

"What's wrong?" I asked. (I was clueless to how I had devastated him. Though what I said was not wrong, my tone was loud and harsh.) "Dad, I'm so sorry. I didn't mean to let you down. I'm sorry I disappointed you."

"Whoa," I said. "You are not a disappointment to me. I was wrong to raise my voice at you. I'm sorry. Please forgive me. By the grace of God, I'll never raise my voice at you again." That moment changed his life. It kept Satan from using unforgiveness to destroy the Word of God in his heart (Matthew 18:34, 2 Corinthians 2:11).

Another time, when our oldest was about six years old, we were celebrating the holidays with Sue's parents. I disciplined him for something but did so harshly and had to apologize. We both wept over it, and you know, I hardly remember him ever disobeying me after that. He never rebelled or questioned me through his teenage years. It was miraculous. My harshness could have damaged him for the rest of his life. It could have created an estranged relationship between us, but repentance changed that trajectory.

We all need to be quick to forgive and quick to repent. It is an attribute of God's love. I Corinthians 13 lists all sixteen attributes of God's agape love. It tells us what real love looks like and how it acts. It says, *"Love suffers long and is kind; love does not envy; love does not parade itself, is not puffed up; does not behave rudely, does not seek its own, is not provoked, thinks no evil; does not rejoice in iniquity, but rejoices in the truth; bears all things, believes all things, hopes all things, endures all things. Love never fails"* (vs. 4-8). What a list!

This is the way God loves us. And because His love resides in us, this is how we ought to love each other. Teaching this to your children will not only protect them from counterfeit loves but help them love their own families when they leave your home.

Chapter 10 | BLESSING OUR CHILDREN

The blessing of the Lord, it maketh rich, and he addeth no sorrow with it.

Proverbs 10:22, KJV

We need to understand the blessing of the Lord so we can be a blessing to others and learn to bless our children. The blessing of the Lord makes us rich. But notice that riches aren't the blessing. The blessing is an intangible thing that affects the tangible. For example, I know people sometimes die and leave an abundance to their children. This is a good thing, unless they never taught their children how to handle wealth. That leads to sorrow. It could even destroy them. God's blessing is not like that. With God's blessing riches flow without sorrow.

The blessing of God is grace or favor. It is God's acceptance, affirmation, and good pleasure toward us (Ephesians 1:3-6). All of us need that affirmation, and we need to learn to give it to our children. When

Jesus received the blessing of His Father at baptism, *"This is my beloved son in whom I'm well pleased,"* it jumpstarted His ministry (Matthew 3:17). Affirmation from a father is powerful. Your children need to know you are pleased with them. Many people live their entire lives seeking and never obtaining their parent's affirmation (especially their faither's). Make sure your children know you are pleased with and proud of them.

God's promises are also His blessings. When God blessed Abram in Genesis 12, He did so by making a promise based on His character, not Abram's conduct. This allowed God to perform the promise on Abram's behalf (Romans 4:13). In Christ, God fulfills all His promises this way (2 Corinthians 1:20). All we have to do is believe. What a blessing!

SPEAK A BLESSING

Blessings are given through words. In Numbers, God told Moses to explain this concept to Aaron so he could bless Israel: *"This is the way you shall bless the children of Israel. Say to them: 'The Lord bless you and keep you; the Lord make His face shine upon you, and be gracious to you; the Lord lift up His countenance upon you, and give you peace.' So they shall put My Name on the children of Israel, and I will bless them"* (vs. 6:22-27). God speaks blessings over us, and we must speak blessings—words of love, favor, honor, and God's promises—over our children so that He can bless them.

What we say and pray over our children matters. Proverbs 18:21 (KJV) says, *"Death and life are in the power of the tongue: And they that love it shall eat the fruit thereof."* Words bless and words curse; they bring life or death. Let's speak life over our children and bless them.

THE BLESSING OF TOUCH

The blessing of God is also given through touch, or the laying on of hands. (This is also how the anointing is transmitted.) When Jesus received the little children in Mark 10, Scripture says, *"He took them up in His arms, laid His **hands** on them, and blessed them"* (vs. 16). At this same time, Jesus was correcting His disciples and telling them that to enter God's Kingdom, we need the faith of a child.

This "laying on of hands" is how Moses blessed Joshua before he died (Numbers 27:18-23). It is how Jacob blessed his grandsons Ephraim and Manasseh (Genesis 48:9-20). It is also how Paul blessed a young pastor named Timothy. In 2 Timothy 1, Paul said to Timothy, *"Therefore I remind you to stir up the gift of God which is in you through the laying on of my hands"* (vs. 6). Paul was referring to the time Timothy was anointed and prophesied over in I Timothy 4:14. As parents, we are in charge of laying hands on our children and speaking blessings over them. We can do this anytime, but an easy way to build this practice into your family routine is to pray over them at night. Lay hands on them in their beds and speak God's promises over them.

ABRAHAM – ISAAC – JACOB

In ancient times, the blessing was viewed as a finite thing. It could only be given to one person in the family—typically, the heir, the eldest son. In Genesis 12, God blessed Abraham, who in turn, blessed his son Isaac. Though not Abraham's firstborn, Isaac was the promised seed. He was the child of faith. Without the fulfillment of God's promise, Abraham and Sarah could not get pregnant. Sarah suggested Abraham use her handmaid in order to have children. Abraham agreed and sired Ishmael. Ishmael was born of the flesh, the work of man, and we are still dealing with those consequences today. Eventually, Abraham returned to faith in God's promise of a son by Sarah, and Isaac was born. Isaac carried the faith of Abraham in his heart, so Abraham gave him the blessing.

Isaac had two sons: the twins, Jacob and Esau. Esau, who was born first, had no desire for the things of God. He sold his birthright for a bowl of soup. Later, as Isaac lay dying, Jacob and his mother, Rebekah, deceived Isaac into giving the blessing of the firstborn to him instead of Esau (Genesis 27:21-29). When Esau heard his father had given Jacob the blessing *"he cried with an exceedingly great and bitter cry [...] "Bless me—me also, O my father!"* (vs. 34). Jacob, on the other hand, learned the lesson and did something different with his blessing. As a man of faith, he passed the blessing on to all twelve of his sons! God used that blessing to charter a nation and make Jacob's sons into the twelve tribes of Israel.

Like Esau, I believe that today, young and old alike are crying out for their father's blessing. When that blessing is withheld, especially in youth, it breaks the spirit of a child and causes great sorrow. Those children grow up still craving their father's blessing. They seek approval from others and are unable to properly relate to a loving Heavenly Father. Thank God, Christ redeemed us from the curse of the law so that the blessing of Abraham might be ours by faith (Galatians 3:13-15). Let's use that blessing to bless our children.

CONCLUSION

Sue and I count raising our children as the highest honor and calling of our lives. Now watching them raising our grandchildren in the nurture and admonition of the Lord is such a blessing. While we made our share of mistakes, we have seen God bring beauty out of ashes and work all things together for our good (Rom. 8:28). Let me encourage you that conviction from God calls us up to receive His loving corrections to be the best parents we can be. Do not receive the guilt or condemnation of Satan pulling you down and away from God. Conviction always involves God calling us up to a better way and closer to Him. Condemnation is Satan pushing us down and away from God's loving arms.

"Father, I pray for every parent to be the parent You have called them to be. Give them the grace to prepare their children for a life of blessing and success. In Jesus' name, Amen."

SALVATION PRAYER

If your heart desires connection with your Heavenly Father and to live in the blessing of His family, there is hope in Christ Jesus. If you have not made Jesus Lord of your life but would like to do so, you can simply pray this:

> *"Father, I come to you today; I confess I'm not right, but I want to be right and make things right. I cannot do enough or quit enough to save myself, I need help. I believe Jesus is that help. I believe He came to this earth, lived a perfect life, and died on the cross for me. He bore my sins and the punishment for all my sins. He died, was buried, and rose again on the third day. I now confess Him as Lord, King, and Savior. Thank you for forgiving me and cleansing me of all my sin and changing me in my heart. Help me now to serve you all the days of my life, with all my heart. Amen!"*

If you prayed this prayer and received Jesus in your heart today, let us know and we will send you a free book! Contact us at 580-634-5665 or dsm@pastorduane.com

GRACE & TRUTH

Join Duane as he boldly teaches Biblical wisdom mixed with his unique sense of humor, offering hope & revelation for today's world.

ABOUT THE AUTHOR

Duane Sheriff has been in ministry for over four decades. He is an author, international apostolic teacher, conference speaker and founder of Victory Life Church. He is known for his humor and ability to present the Gospel with clarity and simplicity. He is passionate about helping people discover their identity and grow in Christ through his unique biblical insights.

His first book, *Identity Theft*, was released in 2017. Since then, he has authored several more books including: *Divine Guidance, Rhythms of Grace, Blessing Your Children, Erasing Offense, Counterculture, Better Together and Our Union with Christ.* He also serves as an adjunct instructor at Charis Bible School, and hosts "Grace & Truth," a daily television broadcast. Duane and his wife, Sue, were married in 1980 and have four children, who have blessed them with numerous grandchildren.

For additional study resources or free teachings visit our website at **www.pastorduane.com**

CONTACT INFORMATION

Duane Sheriff Ministries

PO Box 427, Durant, OK

dsm@pastorduane.com

Helpline (Mon. – Fri. 8am-5pm CT)

580-404-0376

www.pastorduane.com

Made in the USA
Monee, IL
30 July 2025